TOPIARY IN THE GARDEN

JENNY HENDY

LORENZ BOOKS

This edition is published by Lorenz Books,
an imprint of Anness Publishing Ltd, Hermes House,
88–89 Blackfriars Road, London SE1 8HA
tel. 020 7401 2077; fax 020 7633 9499

www.lorenzbooks.com; www.annesspublishing.com

If you like the images in this book and would like to
investigate using them for publishing, promotions or
advertising, please visit our website www.practicalpictures.com
for more information.

UK agent: The Manning Partnership Ltd
tel. 01225 478444; fax 01225 478440
sales@manning-partnership.co.uk

UK distributor: Grantham Book Services Ltd
tel. 01476 541080; fax 01476 541061;
orders@gbs.tbs-ltd.co.uk

North American agent/distributor: National Book Network
tel. 301 459 3366; fax 301 429 5746; www.nbnbooks.com

Australian agent/distributor: Pan Macmillan Australia
tel. 1300 135 113; fax 1300 135 103;
customer.service@macmillan.com.au

New Zealand agent/distributor: David Bateman Ltd
tel. (09) 415 7664; fax (09) 415 8892

Publisher: Joanna Lorenz
Executive Editor: Caroline Davison
Senior Editor: Lucy Doncaster
Designer: Lucy Doncaster
Photographer: Steven Wooster
Production Controller: Pirong Wang

ETHICAL TRADING POLICY

At Anness Publishing we believe that business should be conducted
in an ethical and ecologically sustainable way, with respect for the
environment and a proper regard to the replacement of the natural
resources we employ.

As a publisher, we use a lot of wood pulp to make high-quality paper
for printing, and that wood commonly comes from spruce trees. We are
therefore currently growing more than 750,000 trees in three Scottish
forest plantations: Berrymoss (130 hectares/320 acres), West Touxhill
(125 hectares/305 acres) and Deveron Forest (75 hectares/185 acres).
The forests we manage contain more than 3.5 times the number of trees
employed each year in making paper for the books we manufacture.

Because of this ongoing ecological investment programme, you, as our
customer, can have the pleasure and reassurance of knowing that a tree is
being cultivated to naturally replace the materials used to make the book.

Our forestry programme is run in accordance with the UK Woodland
Assurance Scheme (UKWAS) and will be certified by the internationally
recognized Forest Stewardship Council (FSC). The FSC is a non-government
organization dedicated to promoting responsible management of the
world's forests. Certification ensures forests are managed in an
environmentally sustainable and socially responsible way. For further
information about this scheme, go to www.annesspublishing.com/trees

Previously published as part of a larger volume, *A Practical Guide to Topiary*

PUBLISHER'S NOTE

Although the advice and information in this book are believed to be accurate and
true at the time of going to press, neither the authors nor the publisher can accept
any legal responsiblity or liability for any errors or omissions that may be made
or for any resulting injury, damage or loss to persons or property as a result of
carrying out any of the projects. Readers should follow all recommended safety
procedures and wear the correct protective goggles, gloves and clothing.

NOTE TO READER

Each of the entries in the plant directory has been given a hardiness rating (for
European readers) and a zone range (for readers in the United States):-

Hardiness Ratings

Frost tender Plant may be damaged by
temperatures below 5°C (41°F).

Half hardy Plant can withstand
temperatures down to 0°C (32°F).

Frost hardy Plant can withstand
temperatures down to -5°C (23°F).

Fully hardy Plant can withstand
temperatures down to -15°C (5°F).

Plant Hardiness Zones

The Agricultural Research Service of the U.S. Department of Agriculture has developed a
system of plant hardiness zones. Every plant in the Plant Focus section has been given a
zone range. The zones 1–11 are based on the average annual minimum temperature. In the
zone range, the smaller number indicates the northernmost zone in which a plant can survive
the winter and the higher number gives the most southerly area in which it will perform
consistently. Bear in mind that factors such as altitude, wind exposure, proximity to
water, soil type, snow, night temperature, shade and the level of water received by a
plant may alter a plant's hardiness by as much as two zones.

Zone 1 Below -45°C (-50°F)
Zone 2 -45 to -40°C (-50 to -40°F)
Zone 3 -40 to -34°C (-40 to -30°F)
Zone 4 -34 to -29°C (-30 to -20°F)
Zone 5 -29 to -23°C (-20 to -10°F)
Zone 6 -23 to -18°C (-10 to 0°F)

Zone 7 -18 to -12°C (0 to 10°F)
Zone 8 -12 to -7°C (10 to 20°F)
Zone 9 -7 to -1°C (20 to 30°F)
Zone 10 -1 to 4°C (30 to 40°F)
Zone 11 Above 4°C (40°F)

CONTENTS

INTRODUCTION

Many people still imagine topiary to be something practised exclusively by skilled gardeners in the employ of the landed gentry. However, it has always had a folk art following among country people and is rapidly becoming a pastime that is fun and accessible for all.

As an art form topiary has a universal appeal, partly because there are so many styling options. Whether you consider yourself conservative or traditional, avant garde or eccentric, there is a branch of topiary that is tailor-made for you.

It does not matter how small your garden is or how ordinary the setting, there is always room for topiary. It can be grown in pots and some of the tall, slender shapes take up very little room. You do not even need to plant from scratch because existing shrubbery and hedging can often be reshaped and sculpted according to your whim.

Another less obvious factor that draws even novice gardeners to topiary is the sheer pleasure associated with clipping and training something wild and untamed, to create order out of chaos and to see the desired

shapes gradually emerging or being further perfected. Neatness freaks beware – this can be an addictive pastime! The fact that architectural elements and statuary can be 'constructed' or 'sculpted' purely from plants is also something to be marvelled at. There are also some financial benefits of topiary: provided you have a degree of patience, you can include substantial features such as green walls, archways and colonnades that would cost significantly more to build from dressed stone or bricks and mortar.

The first mention of topiary can be found in the writings of Roman natural historian and scientist Pliny the Elder (AD62–110) who described fanciful and elaborate elements in his Tuscan garden. Topiary spread far and wide with the advances of the Empire, and some archaeological evidence still remains. At the Roman palace gardens of Fishbourne in Sussex, in England, the pattern of a beautifully ornate box hedge has been revealed.

During the Dark Ages, topiary was still practised but only within monastic gardens and castle defences. Then the 14th century saw the dawn of the Italian Renaissance, which drew inspiration from classical times and profoundly influenced European garden style. Two of the most beautifully preserved gardens of this period are found at Villa Lante and Villa d'Este, near Rome.

The formal gardens of the French Renaissance were more imposing, with huge box parterres and avenues lined with hedging that took your eye to some far distant point. Man's dominance over nature was a common

Opposite *This avenue of topiary at the Château du Pin is an example of how impressive topiary gardens in the French Renaissance style can be.*

Right *Simple geometric shapes are easy to produce and, clipped from plants like box that give a fine-textured finish, they look striking against untamed foliage and flowers.*

Below *No garden or courtyard is too small for potted topiary.*

theme and the master of this style was the architect le Notre who was responsible for the gardens of Vaux le Vicomte and Louis XIV's Palais de Versailles in the late 17th century. At the same time, topiary and formality had reached America, and from Williamsburg, Virginia, a simple, ordered style of gardening spread across the colonies.

In Britain, during the Tudor and Elizabethan periods, the knot garden was a popular feature but by the 17th century all manner of curious creatures were also being created in topiary. In the Netherlands, the passion for topiary was reaching fever pitch and when William of Orange took the throne in Britain in 1688 he introduced a lavish style of formal gardening that was much copied by the country's wealthiest citizens. Ultimately, however, the craze for topiary was swept away in a reaction to its excesses and the Landscape Movement went to extraordinary lengths to rid the country of artificiality.

Fashions come and go, and by the 19th century classical formality was beginning to make a comeback. The Victorians created parterres in public parks and gardens and were passionate about colour, filling the patterns with all kinds of vivid bedding plants and exotics.

The more recent resurgence of interest in topiary can be traced to a number of factors. In the 1960s, American gardeners began developing a form of topiary using wire frames covered in moss and creeping plants, and by the late 1980s this type of portable topiary or 'chlorophyll' began to exert an influence across the Atlantic. Appealing to gardeners wanting instant results, chlorophyll is now called mosaiculture and is growing in popularity all over the world.

Opposite *Contemporary garden designers increasingly use abstract topiary forms and green architectural elements in order to create visually exciting shapes and textures.*

Right *A row of lollipop-headed bay standards adds style to this Mediterranean herb garden.*

Another key reason for topiary's new lease of life was the renewed interest in formality and the desire to recreate authentic period gardens during the 1980s and early 1990s. At this time, a number of high-profile historic garden restorations took place across Britain and Europe, and the gardening public became caught up in a wave of nostalgia. Sales of boxwood soared as parterres, knot gardens and potagers sprang up across Britain, and it was only in the late 1990s that the spread of a new and virulent type of box blight dampened enthusiasm.

Topiary today is more a medium for self-expression than a symbol of status. New modernists, including Piet Oudolf and Jacques Wirtz, have restyled the art to complement contemporary settings, sometimes using a combination of solid abstract shapes and billowing cloud formations in place of more traditional elements.

This book explores the widest definition of topiary and includes all kinds of shaped greenery, from hedges and standards to how to create framed ivy topiary. You will find sections on how to incorporate topiary and green architecture, and the different styles that can be created. The final pages introduce some of the most useful plants for topiary. Generously illustrated, this is an inspirational sourcebook for anyone interested in adding topiary or green architecture to their garden.

TOPIARY STYLE

When it comes to choosing a style of topiary for your garden, the age of the house and any significant architectural features can be a useful starting point. Adding one or two signature topiary features to the basic design is often a more workable alternative to making a historically authentic garden. For instance, if you wanted to give a flavour of classical antiquity to a suburban garden, you could flank an entranceway with a pair of large topiary spirals planted in ornate terracotta pots. A mixture of traditional, geometric figures plus billowing free-form topiary would work well in the surrounds of a simply designed building. But if the house is uninspiring and your garden feels rather flat, you could introduce flamboyant flourishes such as a pleached lime allée leading to a bench seat. So, whatever your approach, clipped and trained forms can reinforce the design and create visual drama.

Left *This scene shows how topiary styles can influence the character of a garden – in this case, the design harks back to the Italian Renaissance, albeit on a small scale.*

CHOOSING A STYLE

Classic topiary shapes and structures can create a very different look, depending on how they are combined. Using mixtures of topiary and green architecture with other plants and hard landscaping materials provides endless variations that can alter the character of a garden.

Container-grown topiary is a good example of the way in which clipped shapes can be used to 'tweak' the finished look. Box balls in tall, galvanized planters are perfect in a modern, minimalist design. The same plants grown in weathered clay pots enrich the atmosphere of a country garden and when planted up in ornate terracotta or carved stone add drama to a Renaissance-style terrace.

However, you do not have to stick to any 'rules' or go for historical accuracy. Topiary can be a useful vehicle for introducing features that technically belong to a different period or style, purely for dramatic effect. There is no reason, for example, why you could not include a

parterre in a hi-tech urban courtyard – perhaps using brightly coloured glass chips as infill in place of traditional gravel. Why not clip go-with-the-flow greenery around the margins of an old stone fisherman's cottage? This new-style topiary technique can be used to reflect the wild landscape and even capture qualities of the sea and cloudscape. When developing a formal garden around a period property, you can create the required ambience or look by adding a few key elements of green, structural planting. These can be used to outline the edges of lawns and pathways, highlight changes in level and emphasize entrances within the garden. The strategic placement of elements such as box balls, cones or spirals can have a truly atmospheric effect.

If no particular style or historical period appeals and you'd prefer to fly in the face of convention, then why not make your garden into a unique artistic statement and expression of your own individuality using elements of green sculpture, as topiary aficionados have been doing for centuries.

Opposite *The grounds of this country manor house are underpinned with a formal plan, the pathways defined and punctuated with softly rendered and repeated cones.*

Left *An alternating row of large clipped domes and cake stands helps strengthen the boundary of this formal garden, which is emphasized by the shaped lawn edge.*

grand designs

The gardens of the Italian and later French Renaissance had a profound effect on gardens in the rest of Europe, with the wealthy, privileged classes creating horticultural extravaganzas designed solely to impress. The stunningly theatrical gardens of Louis XIV at Versailles proclaimed the Sun King's dominance over nature, and were built on a scale designed to dwarf the visitor and leave them with a sense of awe for the power of the King. Today, you can use the same key elements of geometric formality and symmetry, and manipulate scale and proportion to trick the eye into imagining the space to be larger than it really is.

Topiarized shapes, such as pointed pyramids and cones, spheres and domes, columns and colonnades, were used to create rhythm in Renaissance-style gardens and to punctuate, and strengthen, the ground plan.

These gardens, with so much structure and pattern, did not have to rely on colourful blooms for interest. At Renishaw Hall, in Derbyshire, England, Sir George Sitwell used only white blooms to avoid detracting from the green architecture, statuary, pools and fountains when designing his Italianate garden 100 years ago.

In smaller town and city gardens, you could copy and scale down some of the effects seen at Italian jewels like Villa Lante and Palazzo Farnese, using dwarf hedging to divide the space into geometrically shaped compartments containing lawn, gravel or water. Few people have room to reproduce the intricately wrought French-style parterres shown in pattern books of the period, but it is quite easy to create a small-scale copy or plan a simple, repeating border. Certain props such

Below *Once perfectly balanced and in proportion, these yew pyramids have 'drifted' over time, but there's no mistaking the influence of the Renaissance.*

Below *Grand gardens relied on formality and symmetry to achieve their effect. Here, a modern interpretation of these principles creates similar results.*

Above *Though formal in layout, with clipped hedges and box balls providing additional structure, this delightful country garden has a relaxed atmosphere.*

Right *With the half-timbered wing of the house at the end of this vista, a theatrical stage set has been created to lead the eye and to frame the view.*

as large Italianate terracotta vases or Versailles planters containing spirals or globe-headed standards make an acceptable substitute for classical statuary, and will give your modest patch a flavour of continental grandeur without breaking the bank.

Topiary is a signature of the classic country garden, the structural elements worked in against a backdrop of billowing herbaceous borders and festooning roses. Though the layout of many period properties is formal, the atmosphere can be surprisingly relaxed. The laid-back ambience of formal gardens is often caused by mature topiary gradually losing its crisp shape; in fact, you are more likely to find grand old holly, yew and holm oak (*Quercus ilex*) figures with generous curves than immaculate angles, even if they started out mirroring the carved stonework of the property.

Alleés of pleached lime or stilt hedges made from hornbeam add a more formal note to a main drive and, on larger properties, giant cylinders or turrets can be used to create avenues. But the garden of the country house is ultimately less about show and more about comfort and practicality. To achieve this, the grounds are often divided into smaller, more intimate areas, each bounded by hedging incorporating an arched entranceway. Within each space, low walls of box frame flowers and herbs, and balls and domes define the intricacies of the ground plan.

Knot gardens are rarely cut with the precision reserved for parterres, their interweaving threads often being composed of less well-behaved plants, such as cotton lavender and shrubby thyme, since immaculate clipping might look out of place where the terraces or pathways are weathered and uneven.

cottage topiary

Some of the most remarkable, eye-catching examples of topiary can be found in cottage-style front or back gardens. Owners derive immense pride from creating and maintaining unique shapes and figures, some of which are larger than life and dwarf both the house and its pocket-handkerchief garden. Keep a look out on your travels: besides the familiar animal line-up of rabbits, cockerels, peacocks and so on, it's easy to spot more eccentric, outrageous and wittier kinds of topiary, with some privet hedges even being turned into steam locomotives or dragons. Other gardens take on a fairy-tale or a child-like quality, perhaps adding a Hobbit-style yew house with a pheasant perched on top, or by shaping a large flowering shrub, such as *Viburnum tinus*, into a giant toadstool.

If you want to create a topiary flourish, the main entrance is an ideal location. Sometimes you'll see a picket gate flanked by a pair of enormous holly finials that have long since blocked the way in, while a hardy, native, hawthorn hedge is often trained up and over a gate to form an arch.

In traditional gardens, a straight, central path, which might be flanked by a neat dwarf lavender or hyssop hedge, leads to the front porch. Standards trained from cuttings or self-sown seedlings, and planted in simple clay pots or wooden barrels, are often used to embellish the front door. Plants with fragrant flowers or aromatic foliage, such as rosemary, lavender and myrtle, are particular favourites. You might also find potted ivy topiaries on simple frames shaped into hearts or chickens.

Opposite *Neat topiary hedges flank the path leading to the front door of the cottage, and a domed cake stand marks the corner of the lawn.*

Left *Different animal shapes, such as this rabbit, are especially suited to cottage gardens.*

Below *This charming little window in a hedge, complete with windowbox, is flanked by two gold-leaved standards.*

courtyard topiary

With the right plants, décor and a bubbling fountain or classical statue, a bare courtyard of bricks and concrete can be transformed into an oasis of greenery. Geometric pieces of topiary act like sculpted stone and, in a space dominated by the surrounding architecture, make a wonderfully bold, theatrical statement.

If the ground is concrete then topiary must be containerized and most species, with the exception of yew, can be successfully kept in pots. Choose containers to strengthen your design, using anything from traditional, Italianate terracotta to modern galvanized metal. While the light in a courtyard may be a limiting factor, many plants, including box, ivy and holly, will thrive in shade. And because of the extra shelter, you may also be able to keep more tender plants outdoors all year round.

A pair of potted topiaries is ideal for highlighting an entrance, and groups of diverse shapes are perfect for decorating awkward corners. Try combining them with pots of annual flowers and bulbs for seasonal highlights, or add a few elegant flowering standards, such as fuchsias, abutilons or marguerite daisies.

Water is an essential ingredient for a courtyard garden. Semi-circular, raised-wall pools are ideal where space is limited but a central pool evokes an atmosphere of tranquillity. Enclose it within low clipped hedging or outline it with dwarf box balls in identical pots. Make the most of space by growing upwards and covering bare walls. Ivy can be trained to cover shaped trellis panels or rope swags, the latter creating a sense of rhythm around your outdoor room. Espalier-trained shrubs like firethorn (*Pyracantha*) are also effective and take up little room.

Opposite *A formal courtyard, with box hedging and clipped box standards in terracotta pots, is a study in elegant simplicity.*

Above *The bold symmetry of this beautifully planted walled garden is emphasized by the large golden cones and their tiny potted replicas.*

Left *Potted topiary columns and standards can be placed around a terrace or courtyard in order to create height and drama.*

modern classics

The architectural and almost machine-made qualities of some geometric pieces of topiary make them ideally suited for use in modern minimalist landscapes, which often have a rectilinear ground plan. The resulting simplicity of such a design generates a soothing ambience and a serene space.

Domes, spheres, pyramids, cones and blocks are typically used in contemporary gardens, with clipped evergreens usually taking precedence over more colourful annual or perennial blooms, and the palette is restricted mainly to shades of green with perhaps touches of grey or bronze. Interesting combinations of topiary elements include neat evergreen groundcover, ornamental grasses and sculptural plants such as phormiums and yuccas. Two of the hallmarks of contemporary landscaping are purity of line and a

sense of space, so it is vital that topiary and green architecture, such as formal hedges, are arranged with sensitivity, particularly with regard to scale and proportion. 'Less is more' is an extremely useful guide. Still pools and other reflective surfaces, including glass and polished metal, can be effectively employed in order to enhance the modern topiary garden in the daytime, while at night spotlights, and even coloured floodlights, can provide drama and excitement.

Sometimes topiary is used like a piece of stone sculpture to create the focal point at the end of a vista, but asymmetry is more usual and it is the mathematical forms, the lines and angles that intrigue.

One of the most radical developments in topiary in recent years has been the use of free-flowing, organic shapes. This style of naturalistic contouring is striking

Below *This architectural garden uses a series of angular shapes to create a structured feel.*

Below *Mixing traditional and avant-garde elements can be highly effective in garden design.*

Above *Hanging over the water, this cloud-pruned tree adds a sense of timelessness to the scene, its shape reminiscent of an aged, wind-blasted pine.*

Right *The reflections in the pools enhance this structured garden of modern formality. Note how the box squares echo the shape of the trellis panels against the wall.*

when contrasted with crisp architectural elements, such as hedges, formal pools and the walls of buildings, and it also works well as textured groundcover in more relaxed or less intensively cultivated areas of the garden.

The influence of the East is apparent in the billowing, cloud-like forms that have become fashionable for adding a touch of urban chic to city gardens and roof terraces in recent years. This style of freehand clipping is highly adaptable and you can have great fun experimenting, seeing what shapes emerge, and if you have a mature and perhaps slightly overgrown shrub border or unruly mixed hedge you could begin clipping right away. To achieve a more uniform look in terms of texture and colour, however, it is advisable to start from scratch by planting in blocks using just one subject such as box.

Plants can also be clipped separately, producing something resembling a basket of eggs, but it is more usual to allow them to fuse, creating an undulating surface of miniature hills and valleys. New wave topiarists also specialize in hedges, screens and other 3-D structures. Although the shapes may be quite stylized, inspiration is often derived from the natural world – from waves, snail spirals and curling tendrils, for example.

Another exciting development is the contouring of the ground to make turf-covered earthworks. These look most effective in large, open areas and the designs often in some way reflect, or are sympathetic to, the surrounding landscape. More static, geometric landforms suit minimalist, rectilinear designs. Based on ancient symbols, turf labyrinths have also become popular features of New Age gardens.

DESIGNING WITH TOPIARY

Topiary is an incredibly versatile medium, which can help to create the structure of the garden as well as adding decorative sculptural elements. The contrast between the artificiality of topiary and the surrounding natural forms of the garden is central to its appeal. Depending on your approach, results can be theatrical and dramatic, or flowing and organic, the clipped greenery catching the light and often producing dramatic shadows that enliven the atmosphere of the garden.

Topiary can also be used to create patterns and designs of varying complexity, to set up pleasing visual rhythms and highlight existing features. You can even use topiary to produce a sense of depth and perspective, and to create the illusion that the space is much larger than it really is. Used skilfully it can manipulate our perception of the space surrounding the house.

Left *These magnificent yew pyramids make an imposing feature in this formal garden, and have the look of fortifications, visually strengthening the boundary wall.*

FORM AND FUNCTION

Garden design is a combination of aesthetics and practicality; in other words we want the space to look beautiful but we also want it to have a satisfactory structure. One of the key tools for achieving both aims is green architecture – topiary and hedging.

Living architecture includes walls, pillars, arches and entranceways as well as sculpture. These elements literally grow up from the lines of the ground plan and help define the limits and functions of different areas within the garden, as well as providing privacy. Without them, gardens can seem flat and featureless, far too open and lacking depth and textural contrast. This is especially true in winter when the majority of taller, structural herbaceous plants and climbers have died back down to ground level, and the deciduous shrubs have lost their leaves.

Even relatively relaxed, informal plots, which rely heavily on flower and foliage colour, can benefit from a few strategically placed pieces of topiary. The classic cottage garden is a particularly good example. Typically, it has borders to either side of a central path, filled with a seemingly haphazard mix of flowers, herbs and vegetables, but adding a few topiarized shrubs (possibly including an arched entrance of trained greenery) provides an overall shape or pattern and links different elements of the plot together.

Evergreens, such as holly and yew, are clipped into simple shapes within borders, while paths and flower beds may be framed with dwarf hedging of lavender or box to frame the exuberant planting behind, making the space feel less 'busy'.

In formal designs, a large proportion of the 'bones' of the garden may be fashioned from topiary, but this technique isn't restricted to traditional garden styles or the grounds of period properties. Many contemporary designers incorporate geometric topiary pieces and formal hedging into minimalist or avant-garde spaces where the look relies on clean lines and solid, well-defined shapes contrasting with open spaces or voids in the form of lawns, pools or paving.

Left *Here, the clever use of box-edged compartments and luxuriant wall planting eases the transition between house and garden.*

Opposite *Formal yew hedging encloses sections of the garden and at key points is clipped into substantial pillars that draw the eye.*

hedges, blocks and steps

Hedges can be viewed as garden barriers, divisions or enclosures, as well as living substitutes for walls and fences. Although labour intensive, they have significant aesthetic advantages over brick and stone.

Hedges make a restful garden backdrop and those with a smooth, clipped, vertical surface provide a perfect foil for decorative flowers and foliage. When neatly maintained and cut to a variety of eye-catching designs and profiles, green masonry can also dramatically enhance the structural lines of the garden.

At their simplest, formal hedges are cut with straight sides, a flat top and right-angle corners, all easily achievable with a long straight piece of wood, spirit level and plumb line. On a sloping site, you can step down the profile of the hedge in stages. A sloping face, known as a batter, with the base wider than the top, allows light to fall evenly, thereby preventing the bottom of the hedge from becoming threadbare. Poorly maintained hedges tend to develop the opposite profile and have a pronounced overhang which robs the base of light, causing bottom growth to be poor and patchy. Imaginative designs might incorporate rococo curves, castellations, buttresses and finials. You can make a wooden template to help snip out patterns, though most gardeners eventually end up doing this by eye, which is much quicker.

Below *Pleached screens and hedges raised on stilts trained from lime, box and hornbeam are perfect where space for planting is at a premium, as in this garden.*

Below *The length of this hedge makes it an impressive architectural feature, containing, as it seems to do, the froth of flowers and other plants that are spilling over the edge.*

Above *Here, a darker yew finial appears to sit on top of stepped box blocks, thus creating an interesting contrast of textures.*

Left *Geometric topiary elements such as these need precision clipping to be successful.*

Electric or petrol hedge trimmers are especially good for large runs, provided they are rested periodically to prevent the motor from burning out, and are properly maintained. When hand clipping with shears, alleviate the strain on your wrists by keeping one hand still, while working with the opposite arm, and then swap over. Also use a long bamboo cane to flick debris from the top of the hedge because, if left, it can lead to fungal infections. Mobile platforms and ladder stabilizers may be a worthwhile investment, especially for maintaining tall hedges.

Square and rectangular blocks help to create an avant-garde look in the garden, perfect for minimalist urban spaces, but these topiarized shapes are some of the most difficult to create and maintain because even the smallest mistake shows up as a glaring error.

Rectangular blocks can be used to create a plinth effect around a statue or sculpture, giving it more prominence. They can also be used like pieces of modern art, set in isolation on a lawn, or to frame a formal pool.

In contemporary gardens, blocks can be embellished by having a simple shape, such as a wooden, metallic or stone pillar, rising out of the centre, while combining contrasting plants can also create an eye-catching effect. Consider, for example, using a square frame of golden yew with a block of dark green yew rising up from the centre. This is quite easy to achieve by planting a solid grid of dark yew surrounded by a row of less vigorous golden yews. On a smaller scale, try a block of box (*Buxus sempervirens*) with a frame of the cream-variegated *B. s.* 'Elegantissima'.

Blocks don't have to be square or rectangular. You can create rhomboids, trapezoids and cheese wedges or design a chess set, sundial or starburst sculpture. You can even create a not-to-be-used flight of steps to link a lower garden with an upper terrace or deck. Fine-leaved box is ideal. Plant right across the area, spacing the young plants evenly. Grow them to the same height and then, using a series of taut lines, begin to cut steps into the block.

doorways, windows, niches and alcoves

Creating shaped apertures in a formal hedge – from circular windows to grand, classically styled arches – strengthens the illusion that the green 'wall' is actually a substantial piece of architecture. Such elements also relieve the monotony of an otherwise featureless hedge by providing a focal point. The glimpse of another garden creates a sense of space within an enclosed area, while a hedge perforated by a series of vertical slits allows light through while maintaining a degree of privacy. Windows or clairvoyées, as they once were known, engender an air of mystery by allowing tantalizing views of the landscape beyond.

A window can often be made just by cutting a hole through the hedge, perhaps capitalizing on a thin patch of branches. Simple shapes, for example circles, ovals and rectangles, are the easiest kind to maintain, and you can use a plywood template attached to a stake for initial training.

In a classically inspired formal garden, the creation of niches and alcoves provides elegant spaces where statuary, obelisks, flower-filled vases, seats and other objects may be highlighted. A shallow niche can usually be clipped out of a mature hedge provided the growth is quite dense and uniform. Take care with quick-growing conifers such as X *Cupressocyparis leylandii* which may not regenerate well if you cut back to the brown inner branches. Niches are particularly interesting when the face of the hedge has a batter or slope to contrast with its perpendicular shape. Clip the shape to the required size to comfortably accommodate the object in question.

A rectangular niche is the easiest shape to attempt, for which you'll only need a plumb line, straight edge and spirit level. Otherwise make a template or use a can of water-based spray paint to mark the shape on the hedge. Niches in a period setting look more authentic with an elegantly curved top – perfect for featuring standards in terracotta pots. For a really eye-catching feature, you could add evergreen pillars or columns at the side. Niches can also be left empty; one by itself looks like a mistake, but a repeating pattern creates textural variation in a long, flat-faced hedge of beech or yew, for example. Large, semi-circular alcoves, known as exedrae, should be planned at hedge-planting time.

When making a shelter for a bench seat, instead of carving your way deep into a hedge, you could simply grow out the sides and top to form an arbour. A rustic-style arbour cut from a hedge of holly, hawthorn or privet is ideal in a country or cottage garden. To speed up the process, you can also plant to the front of the hedge, forming the left- and right-hand verticals and training the branches up to form the arched roof.

Above *A gothic-arched doorway shapes the view at one end of a long topiary avenue that lines up perfectly with the château.*

Opposite *Conifers such as thuja and cupressus make dense, narrow forms. These two columns have been crossed over and tied together below the growing points, resulting in an architectural arch.*

Right *Deep curving exedrae such as this are planned from the beginning of the garden's design. Here, the curved yew bay makes an ideal setting for a piece of sculpture.*

knots and parterres

The Elizabethans were fascinated by complex, intertwining patterns including knots, puzzles and artfully combined initials. They can be found in period buildings in the form of carved wood and plasterwork panels, as well as in costume detail such as embroidered fabrics and ruffs. In the garden, there was an opportunity to design living knots using many familiar herb garden plants, including lavender, cotton lavender (*Santolina*), wall germander (*Teucrium chamaedrys*), hyssop, shrubby thyme, marjoram, pennyroyal (*Mentha pulegium*) and box, all clipped to form low hedges.

Symmetrical designs, such as an overlaying of circles and squares, are relatively easy to create and, today, the choice of plants is much wider. As well as variegated box cultivars you can use forms of Japanese holly, such as *Ilex crenata* 'Golden Gem', varieties of *Euonymus fortunei* (especially 'Emerald Gaiety' and 'Emerald 'n' Gold'), and the purple-leaved dwarf barberry (*Berberis thunbergii f. atropurpurea* 'Atropurpurea Nana').

When clipped with precision, the differently coloured plants appear to weave in and out, under and over. This is pure illusion, of course, a result of making parts of the latticework slightly higher where they cross over.

Above *This parterre consists of box hedge borders creating a circular centre with an inner ring path, four access paths and an outer path.*

Right *The complex, curling patterns of a knot can be defined with colourful plants like lavender.*

Opposite *This stunning parterre at the Chateau de Villandry shows just how effective this type of topiary can be on a large scale.*

This style works well when the hedges are shaped to give a rounded profile. Although the spaces are sometimes filled with plants, the Elizabethan method of using coloured earth shows the pattern most clearly, and is easier to maintain. There is now a wide choice of aggregates, including fine gravel and coloured stone chippings.

Unlike the knot garden, the parterre consists of shapes, outlines or compartments that are separate. Several distinct styles of parterre developed over time, some rigidly geometric, others very flamboyant. The parterre de broderie consisted of elegant motifs that were inspired by flowers, leaves and curling tendrils, mostly fashioned from clipped dwarf box. The infilling or highlighting of parterres was usually done with coloured earth, crushed stone or turf, the latter painstakingly cut by hand.

Some techniques were highly labour intensive, including the arabesque forms of cutwork-in-the-English-manner, with shapes being carved out of lawn and infilled with coloured aggregate. After the grand parterres inspired by the French Renaissance were stripped away in favour of a more naturalistic landscaping style, the parterre did not make a significant comeback until the Victorian era when, once again, highly ornate patterns on a dramatic scale became very popular with gardeners. The shapes were filled with brilliantly coloured bedding plants and sub-tropical foliage.

Whatever pattern or technique appeals to you, bear in mind that the greater the complexity of the design, the more important it is that the plants are maintained in excellent health and are regularly clipped and tidied.

pillars and cake stands

Classic topiary obelisks mirror those made from carved stone, having a square cross-section that tapers to a pyramid-shaped top. DIY frames made from dark green stained wood infilled with chicken wire make for easy training and the foliage eventually grows through the mesh to cover it completely. Clip the top into a pyramid or ball shape. With such a strong profile, these structures are ideal for creating focal points in a formal setting, such as at the end of a central path or pergola walkway.

Decorative treillage frames make a bold impression long before the plant inside has started to fill the centre. You can highlight the contrast between the trelliswork and the interior of dark, evergreen foliage by staining or painting the wood in a paler shade. Although it is tempting to use several plants to fill out the base of a large frame

quickly, this is a short-term solution that can lead to problems when the plants at the centre become starved of light. It is far better to use one well-grown plant with a single leading shoot. Yew is ideal, having such a fine-grained finish, but you can also use holly, (*Phillyrea*), or, for warmer climes, Japanese yew (*Podocarpos macrophyllus*). And for especially quick results, try growing a dark green English ivy over the surface of a lightweight metal frame.

One pillar-like plant that requires very little training is the fastigiate or Irish yew (*Taxus baccata* 'Fastigiata') which also has some very attractive golden forms. To keep the column slim and to prevent the branches splaying out, maintain a single leader and cut back any additional leaders that appear around the sides.

Above *The work of an experienced topiary technician, these immaculate cake stands are clipped with mathematical precision.*

Left *These large, domed topiaries are topped with rounded finials which are relatively easy to shape freehand.*

Other topiary creations have a more pronounced modular structure and are reminiscent of totem poles since sections may have contrasting designs. Such structures are usually cut freehand. One of the most simple yet eye-catching looks rather like a tiered cake stand. There are several variations on this theme. If you intend the segments to be close together the structure can often be clipped from an existing column or cone shape provided it has a central stem. Some types of holly, such as *Ilex aquifolium*, naturally produce branches in tiers, which can be clipped to give greater definition.

Below *Like tapering chimneystacks, these topiaries make a change from traditional obelisks or tall narrow pyramids.*

Above *Simple tiered forms with relatively thick sections could be shaped from a mature plant with a central leader.*

spheres and domes

The most popular topiary figures are those with a simple, rounded profile. Not only are they invaluable for establishing a rhythm, framing entrances and defining the ground plan of a formal garden, but they can also be used to add structure and to inject pleasing shapes and textures into a mixed border.

Domes are particularly easy to train, and can be created using a wide range of plants. Some topiarists favour the dome over the sphere because the shape receives even light and therefore does not go bald at the base. Evergreen contenders include the olive-green *Hebe rakaiensis* and box cultivars such as *Buxus microphylla* 'Green Pillow' and *B. sinica* var. *insularis* 'Tide Hill', which have a natural, bun-shaped habit and require very little clipping. Yew and holly are favourites for large domes, but you can also try the quick-growing Portugal laurel (*Prunus lusitanica*) or *Viburnum tinus*. Silver-leaved *Brachyglottis* Dunedin Group 'Sunshine', plain or variegated *Euonymus japonicus* cultivars, bushy camellias and the tender, glossy-leaved *Pittosporum tobira* are good alternatives. For a finer texture, in addition to yew, box, Japanese holly (*Ilex crenata*) and *Ligustrum delavayanum*, there are shrubby honeysuckle (*Lonicera nitida*), small-leaved, evergreen cotoneasters and scented *Osmanthus* x *burkwoodii*. For petite domes, compact lavenders, *Euonymus fortunei* cultivars, myrtle, small-leaved hebes and *Santolina chamaecyparissus* are worth trying.

Box forms like the compact-growing *Buxus microphylla* 'Faulkner' are ideal for producing a fine-textured ball or dome and, in a modern setting, try planting them in tall galvanized pots.

Above *Box balls in terracotta pots are classic topiary icons. A similar, more easily managed shape is the dome, which is less likely to go thin at the base.*

Opposite left *A change from green, these blue* Chamaecyparis *domes mark out the boundary of a little, Italian-style pool garden.*

Opposite right Combining shapes can create more prominent topiary features. Here, a collar has been added to a sphere.

Right *Clipped topiary spheres like this little box ball mimic architectural details such as stone gate post finials, adding a sense of grandeur to even a modest platform.*

pyramids, cones, cylinders and turrets

One of the classic geometric shapes, the cone is simple to produce and extremely versatile. The shape can vary, ranging from slender, sharply pointed types to broad, spreading, blunt-ended creations. The former suit modern architectural gardens, and look striking when repeated and placed equidistantly either in a row or a chequerboard layout. The latter can be used individually or in pairs in a relaxed country-garden setting. Cones work well in containers, and are also frequently used to highlight key points in the garden design.

To shape a cone, begin with a plant that has a single main shoot or leader in the centre, and a generally upright habit. That way the plant will remain balanced during training, and won't break apart or become lopsided. Stand over the plant and step back at regular intervals, clipping the required shape. When trimming and shaping quite radically, it sometimes pays to work in stages, delaying subsequent clippings to allow the plant time to recover and produce a fresh flush of dense, even foliage.

Above *Slender pyramids clipped from yew create an avenue of structure that comes into its own in winter.*

Left *The line of dark yew pyramids in this immaculately kept garden looks stunning against a backdrop of autumn colour, and helps to establish a sight line, leading the eye to the landscape beyond.*

If you are not confident about shaping by eye, either buy a cone-shaped frame to drop over the existing plant and cut off any protruding growth, or create a home-made frame consisting of a wigwam of bamboo canes. The base of each cane is pushed into the earth, and the frame can be removed when the basic shape has been established.

Egyptian-style pyramids make an impressive sight, but the proportions and angles need to be spot on. Start with a drawing or model, and scale up the dimensions so that you have precise figures to follow when constructing the frame. Pyramids made from equilateral triangles will be quite low and squat, but you can also create narrow forms with a sharply pointed top, ideal for creating avenues and vistas. Yew is an excellent choice, but you could also use holly, holm oak or beech, the latter making an interesting colour contrast against surrounding evergreens during the winter months.

Large, cylindrical pieces of topiary were historically used to create imposing avenues, perhaps leading to a point in the distant landscape. But the lone cylinder is a fascinating, eye-catching shape and can become a dramatic focus when dropped into a mixed border full of sculptural foliage plants, or when paired with other geometric forms, such as a pyramid or dome, in a contemporary design.

In fact, an existing plant can sometimes be given a new lease of life by superimposing the well-defined outline of a cylinder on its uneven form. Likely candidates for this treatment include broad conical or columnar conifers, for example the coloured-leaf forms of thuja and chamaecyparis, holly and bay trees. Yew and the holm oak (*Quercus ilex*) – a holly look-alike – are the traditional favourites for large cylinders, but you could also use boxwood, holly or privet (*Ligustrum ovalifolium*). In temperate regions this vigorous hedging privet remains virtually evergreen during mild winters.

Above *In large gardens, you can afford to add substantial structures. Architectural elements, such as this grand avenue of holm oak cylinders, which resemble massive stone pillars, create a powerful sense of drama.*

The cylinder is cut with a flat top. Take care to use a cane to flick off any debris after clipping to prevent the spread of rot. To be absolutely accurate when cutting, check the sides using a plumb line.

A turret is a good variation, and can have straight or slightly tapering sides with a shaped top – imagine a giant pepper pot with a domed or cone-shaped lid. Turrets act like stone fortifications in the garden, set within or at the end of a formal hedge, or used in pairs like sentry boxes to frame an entrance.

spirals and helter-skelters

Spirals have sufficient presence to be used individually, but they also work well as matching pairs, perhaps flanking a front door or another entrance within the garden, and they can even be planted in small groups to great effect. Spirals differ in form quite dramatically, from full-bodied figures with voluptuous curves to those with slender coils which look like a leafy garland twisted around a bare pole.

The slender-coiled kind can be tricky because they take longer to train than the full-bodied kind, which can be clipped almost instantly, and demand more skill from the topiarist. You will often see them grown from relatively quick-growing conifers such as juniper, thuja and chamaecyparis. They also tend to be quite expensive to buy. However, some of these swirling forms are not as difficult to create as you might think.

Below *Spiral topiary can be created in different sizes, which means it can be incorporated in a variety of gardens, including small courtyard spaces or, as here, on a terrace.*

Below *Spirals are dynamic elements that suggest movement. Though often used in pairs to flank a doorway, grouping spirals randomly can create a contemporary look.*

Box is ideal for clipping small to medium-sized spirals in containers, but yew is better for producing large specimens grown in the ground.

When training a spiral, you can put your own individual stamp on to the design because there are several variables. At one extreme there is the squat snail shell which has very broad coils and only a shallow-cut groove. This means that the coils lie on top of each other with no gaps. If you can imagine attaching a string to the tip and pulling upwards to separate the coils slightly, then you have the next variant whereby the coils are set at a more pronounced angle. This angle, coupled with the width of the coils, suggests varying

Above *The lazy coils of a bright green conifer helter-skelter make a wonderful visual contrast with the dark yew blocks and hedges of this highly architectural garden.*

degrees of motion, from lazy turns to dynamic twists. Sometimes a spiral groove is clipped into a column instead of a cone, and you can also create near-horizontal coils clipped to resemble a gentle helter-skelter.

Whatever shape you decide on, do not worry if your spiral is not mathematically perfect or if an existing topiary begins to drift from the original design, with a pronounced lean or unravelling top. Topiary often ends up being quirky or eccentric.

standards

With a shape such as a simple globe, dome, cone or stylized bird, held at the top of a slender stem, the topiary standard is certainly elegant. Whatever the design, topiary standards will add a touch of style to your garden. Consider them as potted sculptures for the terrace; rising up above a sea of planting in the border or paired with an identical twin to frame a gateway. Many gardeners have experience of making standards using quick-growing tender perennials such as fuchsias and marguerite daisies (*Argyranthemum*) and the same techniques are used for creating standards of box, bay, holly and so on.

Potted box standards are ideal for small, suburban gardens because the plants are quite dainty and the thickness and length of the stem stays in proportion to the size of the head. Problems may arise with other plants, such as the small-leaved privet (*Ligustrum delavayanum*), now a popular substitute for box which is only really suitable for tall standards with a relatively large head because the stem is naturally quite stout.

Ideally, start with a rooted cutting that has not yet been 'pinched out'. You might find suitable seedlings in the garden, such as *Viburnum tinus* or holly (*Ilex aquifolium*). Alternatively, buy young plants, such as variegated holly or bay, that have a single unbranched leader tied to a cane. Remove side shoots that form, but for the moment leave any foliage on the stem because this helps strengthen the leg. Once the leader has been trained to a little below the finished height, pinch out the top bud to encourage a head of new shoots to form. Instant standards can also be shaped from a bushy specimen provided you can see that there is a central, reasonably straight stem. The stem of standards trained from scratch can be formed into a corkscrew by winding them around a central pole while still soft and pliable. This is later removed.

Climbers, such as *Plumbago auriculata* and honeysuckle (*Lonicera periclymenum*), can also be turned into standards by plaiting several stems around a permanent cane support and then shaping the head.

Opposite left *The spiral coils of a Cryptomeria cultivar give this conifer standard the appearance of a mop head.*

Opposite right *Here, a ball-headed standard of* Buxus sempervirens *'Elegantissima' rises above carpeting plants, adding light and definition.*

Right *This bay standard's coiled leg was formed by winding the young, developing stem around a support pillar.*

Below *The stem of this tall standard is especially smooth and straight, sitting neatly at right angles to the beautifully clipped hedge.*

SCULPTING TOPIARY

Topiary is an incredibly malleable art form and some of the shapes and methods of training and clipping create sculptural elements that can delight or amaze. Sometimes, as with more free-flowing topiary, the results are entirely abstract. But in other circumstances, such as Eastern cloud pruning, the subjects are definable. Animals are a favourite for green sculpture – either as moss-filled and framed topiaries or clipped by eye. In formal gardens, as well as peacocks and heraldic lions, you might see shrubs shaped in the form of classical vases or urns.

This section of the book contains a selection of illustrated step-by-step sequences that will enable you to perform everyday techniques and create some of the most common topiary shapes, a listing the plants that are best suited to being trained into particular forms, as well as practical hints and tips.

Left *The combination of different geometric shapes creates a striking and dynamic architectural feature in this garden. They resemble stonework in their neat precision.*

Formal hedges have to be cut regularly in order not only to keep them neat and tidy to look at, but also to prevent wayward stems whipping against people as they walk past. Depending on the type of hedging material, they will require from one to four cuts a year.

how to shape and renovate a hedge

1 Begin clipping and shaping formal hedging only once it is well established. Leave conifers to reach a little below the required height before removing the leading shoot. With semi-evergreen privet and broad-leaved evergreens like laurel, however, cut back towards the end of summer.

2 Formal hedging can be maintained with a hedge trimmer, but you should use protective goggles and gloves. Use the hedge trimmer with a wide, sweeping motion, keeping the blade parallel to the hedge to avoid taking out chunks of foliage.

3 Regenerate threadbare or overgrown hedging by cutting hard back into the old wood of plants such as yew, box, *Ligustrum ovalifolium* and beech. Cut one side of the hedge at a time, leaving a year's gap before tackling the other side. Feed and water well.

4 You should regularly strim underneath the hedge, cutting off weeds and grasses, and dig out any self-seeding brambles or alien shrubs or trees.

NOTES
• Most deciduous hedging is planted in the dormant period and cut back by half immediately afterwards to promote dense branching. This process of cutting the hedge back by half may be repeated the following year to encourage plants to knit together.
• To create buttresses, use several evenly spaced plants to cover the base and allow a section at the back to grow taller, while the rest are cut lower in steps or curved segments. Create finials by allowing shoots to grow up from the surface and clip them to shape using a wire former or train them freehand.

An archway is not difficult to form in an existing hedge, although it will take several years for it to grow into its finished form. Do not leave the shaping too long because it is easier to pull the shoots into shape while they are young, and take care not to accidentally trim off the unkempt growth.

how to shape an arch

1 Leave a wider than door-sized gap when planting a hedge, and continue to cut the frame as the hedge grows so that it has straight sides.

2 When the hedge has grown beyond head height, allow up to three strong stems on each side of the hedge to grow out towards each other. Prune the rest of the hedge normally. At first the new growth will look a bit ragged. After one or two years, the shoots will be long enough to bend over to form the framework of the arch.

3 After one or two years, the shoots will be long enough to be trained into an arch. Encourage the shoots at the top to knit together to form a solid lintel. You may want to use a framework of canes to guide the branches across the gap.

4 Use a hedge trimmer to shape the top and vertical surfaces. When shaping screening plants with lax branches or a hedging plant like hawthorn which has an unruly habit, fix branches to an arched metal frame and continue to clip to shape.

NOTES
• The 'doorway' formed by an arch can be an eruption in the line of the hedge if the top is cut as a square or a semi-circle, or it can start some way down the hedge so that the line forms a gentle swell, more like a wave. Choose the type of arch that best suits the style of the garden; more severe lines of square arches suit formal gardens, while the softer approach may be better for an informal garden.
• A beech archway has the advantage that it holds on to its dead leaves throughout the winter, so its shape is still defined.
• If you line up a series of arches, you could create a formal *allée*.

Define motifs such as a series of square-, rectangular- or diamond-shaped panels in a clipped vertical surface by cutting a groove around a template held with tape. Modern patterns include spirals and Celtic symbols. The process is much like carving a piece of masonry.

how to make a surface pattern

1 The undulating form of this hedge suggested an Egyptian eye to the artist. The outer shape was defined with hand shears and the region of the eye itself lightly trimmed to act as a guide. Use secateurs (pruners), sheep shears or small hand shears to provide greater control and precision cutting. Although shallow cuts inevitably disappear quite quickly, this is a fun way to experiment with sculpting. Do not worry if the cuts expose an interior of bare branches. Provided the plant is one that regenerates readily – for example yew or box – it will soon be covered in new leaves.

2 A shallow, v-shaped groove was then cut around the eye and then the pupil was made by snipping out a circular depression. Any bare stems will soon recover but the shape will need regular clipping or it will soon merge into the rest of the hedge. The ideal time to cut is when the surface is resprouting after its last clipping; that way the design will stand out more clearly. You can also create raised surface patterns by carefully clipping around your designated shape so it stands out in relief.

NOTES
• The dense, evenly clipped surface of formal hedging or large topiary pieces can be cut to create patterns in relief. The finer the detail required, the smaller the leaf must be.
• Ivy is ideal for creating fluid shapes because it is evergreen and self-clinging, and responds well to clipping. Make a template for your design using plastic-coated trellis mesh.

SUITABLE PLANTS
• *Buxus sempervirens* (box)
• *Lonicera nitida* (shrubby honeysuckle)
• *Hedera helix* (common ivy)

Unlike symmetrical shapes that are static in nature, spirals have movement. One important point is that you must plan for the eventual size required. You cannot start with a small spiral and grow on a larger, identical version – you'd need to add to the number of coils or merge existing coils and reshape.

how to clip a spiral

1 Start with a cone that has been clipped several times to create dense growth. If you intend to make deep cuts, it should have a single leader from which all the side branches radiate. Tie a piece of string to the top and wind it around in a spiral, angling the string along the diagonal to make a tapering coil. Match the string to natural gaps in the foliage. The number of turns will depend on the height – typically three to five.

2 Use a pair of secateurs (pruners), small hand shears or sheep shears to cut the initial groove using the string as a guide. Go gently at first, working from the top down and trying to keep the bands as even as possible. Work your way to the centre, cutting out any larger branches with the secateurs.

3 Continue to clip, deepening the groove and creating a coil with a rounded profile. Finally, stand the plant in a sheltered environment and provide optimum growing conditions.

4 Clip in spring and late summer to maintain the shape.

SUITABLE PLANTS
Upright growing species and cultivars with fine foliage such as:
- *Buxus sempervirens* (box)
- *Chamaecyparis*
- *Juniperus* (juniper)
- *Laurus* (bay laurel, sweet bay)
- *Taxus baccata* (yew)
- *Thuja*

Buy a mature, dense, bushy plant with a clear upright stem at the centre. This plant must be the correct height for the final standard as it will fill out rather than grow taller. The treatment may seem rather drastic, but the head soon starts to develop ready for further shaping.

● how to train a standard

1 Cut off all the branches emerging from the base to leave one upright stem with side shoots along its length. Remove most of the side shoots up to the base of the proposed head, but retain a few leaf shoots to help the trunk to grow in strength.

2 Begin to shape the head by shortening the side shoots to form a rough ball. Cut out the shoot tip of the leading growth to encourage side shoots to form. Pinch out other shoot tip buds with thumb and forefinger.

3 Tie the stem to a vertical cane that reaches to the base of the ball of shoots. Continue shaping the head to the desired shape as it grows. Give the plant some slow release fertilizer and water well. Stand in a sheltered spot.

4 When clipping the final shape, flip the shears over so that the blades follow the curve of the ball. Continue to pinch off any leaves or shoots that appear on the stem or leg of the standard.

SUITABLE PLANTS
- *Buxus sempervirens* (box)
- *Cupressus* (cypress)
- *Laurus* (bay laurel, sweet bay)
- *Lonicera nitida* (shrubby honeysuckle)
- *Ilex aquifolium* (common holly)
- *Osmanthus* (false or sweet holly)
- *Rosmarinus officinalis* (rosemary)

Though normally associated with Japanese gardens, cloud topiary is found throughout the Far East and is equally a part of traditional Chinese and Thai gardens. There are numerous, subtly different forms of cloud topiary, but they all involve the foliage being clipped into cloud-like shapes.

how to make a cloud topiary

1 Open up the foliage with both hands in order to reveal the framework of branches underneath so you can examine it. An ideal scenario is one or more main stems with strong side branches.

2 Cut out any unwanted branches with secateurs (hand pruners), leaving behind more than you will actually need at this stage. Turn the plant around and stand back regularly to see the shape.

3 Strip the leaves and smaller branches off the main stems that are to be retained using your hands or secateurs. Use bamboo canes and wire to bend some branches into shape.

4 Trim the other branches at the stem tips to encourage compact growth. There should be space between each 'cloud'. Clip once or twice in spring and summer to retain the shape and keep it neat.

SUITABLE PLANTS
- *Buxus sempervirens* (box)
- *Ilex crenata* (Japanese holly)
- *Ilex vomitoria* (Yaupon holly)
- *Ligustrum delavayanum* (privet)
- *Lonicera nitida* (shrubby honeysuckle)
- *Cryptomeria japonica* (Japanese cedar)

Birds, such as chickens, cockerels, pheasants and peacocks, are particularly popular partly because their simple outlines are easily recognized and not out of place in the garden. These shapes are relatively easy to clip and train freehand and can guarantee good results.

● how to make a topiary bird

1 Choose a squat, bushy plant with plenty of dense foliage. Select suitable stems for the head and tail of the bird and tie these together with raffia or string.

2 Set the tail at the desired angle, using string and a tent peg pushed into the ground. Using shears, start shaping the bird by clipping out the foliage between the tail and head stems.

3 Trim the foliage at the sides to create the curve of the bird's body. Shake out the bush as you work to release clippings that may be caught behind others.

4 Using secateurs (pruners), you can then go on to shape the head and neck of the bird. To train the beak, simply twist a small length of garden wire around the soft wood. Again using shears, cut away branches at the bottom of the plant to form the nest. Remember to feed and water the topiary regularly to encourage recovery and take pictures to help you trim it and keep it in shape.

SUITABLE PLANTS
- *Buxus sempervirens* (box)
- *Ilex* (holly)
- *Ligustrum delavayanum* (privet)
- *Lonicera nitida* (shrubby honeysuckle)
- *Podocarpus microphyllus*
- *Taxus baccata* (yew)
- *Thuja*

With most forms of topiary, slow- and compact-growing shrubs are the best to choose. These hold their shapes better and tend to grow at an even pace all over the shape. Avoid large-leaved shrubs as these are difficult to cut into complex shapes.

how to make a topiary pig

1 Ingenuity and creativity are two of the key elements in producing interesting pieces of topiary. Seeing a pig in this box shrub is a stroke of genius.

2 You must have a clear idea of what you are doing before you start clipping. You should work out where all the main elements are going to go.

3 The finished pig makes an eye-catching feature in this winter garden. Unlike a marble sculpture, if you do make a mistake while clipping, you can wait until it grows again and then correct the error. It is a good idea to take pictures of the finished pig from different angles so you can recreate it when it grows out.

4 Once you have achieved the shape you require it is essential that you keep pruning it to that shape. If you leave it too long, shoots will lengthen, often at different rates. If you simply shear off 15cm (6in) all over, you will end up with a distorted shape. Using a photograph as a guide, try to cut back to a regular distance over the whole topiary.

SUITABLE PLANTS
- *Buxus sempervirens* (box)
- *Ilex crenata* (Japanese holly)
- *Ilex vomitoria* (Yaupon holly)
- *Ligustrum delavayanum* (privet)
- *Taxus baccata* (yew)
- *Thuja*

The beauty of ivy topiary is that you can create the impression of classical topiary relatively quickly. Ivy-covered frames work well in pots and are ideal for the smaller garden. Simple frames, such as a 2-D star or heart, can be made from heavy-gauge galvanized wire.

how to make an ivy spiral

1 Select plain green ivy plants, preferably those with long stems in order to achieve quick results. Pick a variety of ivy that has short 'joints' or internodes (that is, the space between the buds). Push the frame into position and then plant the ivies around the rim of the pot so that the stems are next to the base of the frame. The same technique applies to any framed ivy topiary shape.

2 Wind the stems of the ivy plants around the upright struts. There is usually no need to tie them in position since the leaf bases act like grappling hooks. Try to create an even coverage of foliage.

3 As the plants grow, continue to spread out the new shoots until the frame is completely covered.

4 Thereafter, trim off any excess foliage in order to maintain the spiral shape. Feed regularly with liquid fertilizer.

NOTE
When creating a spiral, several stems of ivy are wound around a coil and trained together until they reach the top. For a standard, the stems are twisted together up the main stem and then trained out to cover the head. Finally, the leaves on the leg are pinched off to produce a neat finish.

One of the reasons topiaried ivy is so quick to create is that it only covers the outside of the framework and does not have to form a dense mass in the centre – a bit like making a hollow papier-mâché head as opposed to carving one in solid wood or marble.

how to make an ivy ball

1 Place one wire hanging basket on a flower pot for balance. Line the inside with moistened moss and fill with compost (soil mix).

2 Repeat the process with a second basket. Place the two basket frames firmly together to form a ball shape and tie the two rims together with wire twists. You should now have a secure wire ball filled with moss and compost. Attach three strong chains to the joined edge for hanging the ball.

3 Using a sharpened peg or cane, poke holes in the moss about 2.5cm (1in) apart, moving in a circular direction, starting from the top. Push ivy cuttings into the holes, also moving in a circular direction, starting from the top.

4 Once you have planted most of the ivy cuttings, hang the basket up and finish the underside of the topiary ball, filling in any gaps elsewhere as well. Adjust the cuttings so that they fall nicely and cover the ball.

NOTE
This form of topiary has become popular, and garden centres have responded by offering a good range of differently shaped formers over which to grow the ivy. The better-quality ones are made from thick wire or even steel, while cheaper ones made from chicken wire are available.

TOPIARY PLANTS

Most of the plants in this section share key characteristics. On clipping, the ideal topiary plant will become more densely branched with smaller leaves, resulting in a smooth-textured appearance without unsightly gaps. When cut back hard, either for formative work or during restoration, woody growth should regenerate easily.

Choosing the right plant is essential to the success of your project and the directory lists the relative merits of each of the more popular subjects. You will find a preponderance of evergreen species and cultivars because topiary should have a year-round presence. However, some vigorous deciduous species have been included, since these can make substantial structural elements, such as tall hedges and pleached screens, relatively quickly. Tough, deciduous plants may be preferable in exposed gardens or those experiencing harsh winters.

Left *It is advisable to choose plants that are suited to particular forms of topiary, such as cloud pruning, which requires small-leaved evergreens like box or Japanese holly.*

caring for your plants

TOOLS AND EQUIPMENT

The different pieces of equipment that you will need when topiarizing will depend on the type and scale of topiary that you are planning.

The more expensive tools tend to have blades made out of hardened steel, which does not blunt as quickly. Proper maintenance will prolong the life of your equipment and includes sharpening as well as cleaning and oiling blades after use to prevent rust.

Secateurs (pruners) Use secateurs to trim thin woody stems and soft shoots as well as to shape and maintain large-leaved evergreen topiaries. Bypass secateurs cut more cleanly than anvil types,

Below *The most essential tool for a topiarist is a good pair of secateurs, which should be kept sharp.*

which can squash or bruise the stems. Left-handed types are available and ratchet pruners allow tough stems to be cut in stages without straining your hand.

Long-handled pruners These have more leverage than secateurs, and therefore more cutting power. Use them to cut through thicker stems. Ones with telescopic handles have a greater reach. Do not overstrain – move to a small pruning saw with a curved blade if the branch is too thick to cut through easily.

Shears These are available in different sizes. The smallest, often labelled ladies' shears, have short blades and a narrow 'snout', and are essential for any kind of detailed clipping and shaping. Hedge-cutting shears, with wavy-edged blades, are designed to resist clogging and these are ideal for maintaining large, simple topiary forms. Do not try to clip tough stems with small shears as you risk damaging the blades. Also ensure that the blades of any shears are regularly sharpened. Clean off the sticky sap from the blades as you work. One-handed shears are useful for light trimming. Those such as sheep

Above *Small shears are ideal for detailed clipping as they give you maximum control.*

shears are often sold in connection with topiary, but, as with all one-handed shears and pruners, prolonged use can be tiring.

Hedge trimmers Either electric or petrol-driven, hedgetrimmers are powered by a range of motors and have different blade lengths. The more powerful petrol-driven models suit gardens with a lot of formal hedging or large topiary shapes to maintain, and are useful where there is no convenient power supply. Electric models are lighter. Rest the equipment to avoid burning out the motor and do not tackle material that is too thick for the blades to cut with ease. Clean the blades and replenish the lubricant as required.

PLANT MAINTENANCE

After spending so much time creating your topiary specimens, you should ensure that they are well maintained. Feeding, clipping, repair work and winter protection are all tasks that will need to be undertaken at some stage.

Clipping Check the topiary plants directory on the following pages for ideal timings for clipping. For evergreens, this is generally in spring or early summer, after the risk of frost has passed, and again in late summer. Trim most deciduous plants in the dormant period, but clip spring- and early-summer-flowering standards that bloom on the previous season's growth immediately after flowering.

When clipping rounded shapes, turn the shears over so that the blade follows the curve more easily. If you are unsure about how close to trim, just clip over lightly, then stand back to assess your progress. Before trimming hedging, including parterres and knots, put down ground sheets to collect debris. The removal of clippings helps to prevent disease problems.

Feeding Large topiaries grown in a lawn may not need feeding if the grass is regularly treated with fertilizer. A slow-release granular type, designed for shrubs and roses, and raked in around the base of your topiary pieces in spring, is usually sufficient for plants in the border. The shallow roots of boxwood can be damaged, causing scorching of the foliage if concentrated fertilizer is applied.

Potted topiary Pick a pot that easily accommodates the root system but which is in proportion with the top growth or frame. For long-term container planting, use a soil-based potting mix, perhaps mixed with some peat- or coir-based potting mix to lighten the composition. Cover the drainage holes with crocks or broken pots and/or several inches of coarse gravel to allow excess water to escape. Leave a sufficient gap between the soil surface and the rim of the pot to facilitate watering. Apply liquid feed between mid- to late spring and late summer, and water regularly. Routinely turn pots against a wall so that they receive even light. Top up with fresh potting mix every spring in order to cover any roots that have been exposed.

Renovation and repair Plants can become threadbare or die back in patches, often because of a lack of light or problems with pests and diseases. If the rest of the plant is healthy, cut out all the dead branches and, if necessary, open out the hole to allow in more light. This, combined with feeding and watering, should encourage the dormant buds to sprout and fill in the damage. When old plants get out of shape or fail to produce much new growth, it could mean that they need to be rejuvenated. This involves cutting hard back into the framework of branches.

Winter protection Ideally, move potted topiary within the sheltered environs of the house (e.g. against a warm wall) or, for tender species, under glass. Wrap pots left outdoors with bubble plastic insulation to protect the roots and use horticultural fleece to cover the foliage of types vulnerable to wind scorch. For standards, use foam pipe insulation or lagging to protect the stem. Ensure good drainage by raising up pots on feet or wheeled bases.

Below *Clippings are easier to collect if you lay a plastic sheet along the base of the hedge.*

a-z of topiary plants

Buxus
BOX

A shrubby evergreen with small leaves and a dense branching habit, box is invaluable for topiary. *Buxus sempervirens* has lots of different forms but the species, common box or boxwood, is the most widely used for topiary.

Cultivation Box enjoys slightly alkaline, humus-rich soil and grows well in shade, disliking hot, dry conditions. Pot plants are best fed with dilute liquid feed, while those in the ground thrive with an annual mulch of well-rotted horse manure. Clip in late spring or early summer and again before the end of late summer.

Use glazed pots instead of terracotta because they keep the roots cool and moist. Also use pots whose width exceeds their depth to

Buxus sempervirens 'Marginata'

accommodate the surface roots. When planting a hedge or using several plants to construct a shape, use identical clones.

Varieties Dwarf box (*B. sempervirens* 'Suffruticosa'; hardy/Z 6–9), until recently the most commonly used plant for creating knots and parterres and for edging paths, is highly prone to box blight (*Cylindrocladium*), a disease for which there is, as yet, no cure. Some gardeners now prefer *B. microphylla* 'Faulkner' but it is also susceptible. Hardier alternatives include the slow-growing *B. sempervirens* 'Vardar Valley', *B. sinica* var. *insularis* (hardy/Z 4–9) and *B. microphylla* 'Compacta' (hardy/Z 5–9). Variegated forms include the cream-marbled *B. sempervirens* 'Elegantissima'. Some forms of *B. microphylla*, such as 'Green Pillow', produce a good shape with little training.

Uses Modest hedges; figurative and geometric shapes, including those requiring fine detail; standards; free-form clipping; knots and parterres.

Problems Various box blights, including *Volutella* and *Cylindrocladium*. Destroy infected plants and sterilize

cutting equipment. Healthy box is less susceptible, so provide ideal growing conditions, collect debris after clipping and do not over-clip. Thin the foliage occasionally to allow more light and air to penetrate to the centre.

Box *psyllid* is an insect that causes apical buds to distort and resemble tiny Brussels sprouts. It is not usually serious and can be controlled by clipping, blasting the plants with jets of water or spraying in mid-spring with insecticidal soap. Reddish-brown leaves usually signify stress, such as cold conditions, not enough feed, or excess heat.

Carpinus betulus
COMMON HORNBEAM

Sometimes confused with beech, common hornbeam (*Carpinus betulus*) is a deciduous shrub with broad green leaves. It holds on to its coppery autumn leaves through the winter, making it an ideal choice for formal hedges. It can be pleached or trained over a framework or *treillage*.

Cultivation Hornbeam is weather-resistant and hardy, and grows on most soils in sun or light shade. Prune in early and late summer.

Chamaecyparis

Varieties Common hornbeam (*C. betulus*) and the upright *C. b.* 'Fastigiata'. (Hardy/Z 5–9)

Uses Formal hedging and other large architectural elements, including stilt hedges and pleached screens; tunnels or *berceaux*.

Problems Few

Chamaecyparis
CYPRESS

The familiar hedging conifer, lawson cypress (*Chamaecyparis lawsoniana*), is a vigorous grower, often utilized as a windbreak, especially near the coast.

Cultivation Best on humus-rich, moisture-retentive, alkaline soil. Clip at least twice a year during the growing period, but do not cut back too hard into brown growth because new shoots rarely regenerate from old wood.

Varieties A range of foliage colours; there are slower-growing forms with a narrow, upright habit. (Hardy/Z 6–9)
Uses Geometric figures, large architectural elements, hedges.
Problems Few

Cotoneaster

The small-leaved evergreen, semi-evergreen or deciduous types of prostrate or dome-forming cotoneasters are best. Deciduous *Cotoneaster horizontalis* has structured, fishbone-like branches as well as good autumn leaf colour and usually excellent berries.
Cultivation Hardy and easy to grow, tolerates clay but prefers free-draining soil. Full sun is best but it grows in partial shade. Prune deciduous and semi-evergreen forms in winter. *C. microphyllus* is best clipped after the white blooms have faded and, again, in late summer, or clip in alternate years.
Varieties *C. horizontalis* (hardy/Z 5–9) will cover a north- or east-facing wall. For a tight, close-knit form, use the bushy, dome-shaped *C. microphyllus* (hardy/Z 6–8).
Uses *C. horizontalis* gives semi-formal wall coverage; *C. microphyllus* makes formal domes as well as free-form shapes. Some cotoneasters are trained to make small, weeping standards.
Problems Few

X *Cupressocyparis leylandii* 'Golconda'

x *Cupressocyparis leylandii*
LEYLAND CYPRESS

Loathed by some because of its reputation for growing far too tall and blocking out the light, leyland cypress is a gift for impatient topiarists wishing to make large architectural structures in a hurry. If clipped frequently, it develops a dense, fine-textured appearance.
Cultivation Easily established on most neutral to acid soils, except those that are very dry or waterlogged. Clip frequently when in active growth, but do not cut into brown foliage as old wood rarely regrows.
Varieties Gold-leaved forms, such as 'Castlewellan', 'Gold Rider' and 'Robinson's Gold', are less vigorous than X *Cupressocyparis leylandii*. (Hardy/Z 6–9)
Uses Formal hedging and windbreaks as well as architectural shapes including green colonnades, arches and exedrae. With care, hedges

may be kept to just 30cm (12in) wide. Golden varieties are sometimes used for large, corkscrew spirals.
Problems With poor growing conditions, it is susceptible to fungal diseases such as cankers and soil-borne *Phytophthora*. Hedging plants purchased from nurseries may be pot bound, adversely affecting establishment. Avoid plants over 45cm (18in) tall.

Cupressus
CYPRESS

These large coniferous trees have a conical habit and look statuesque in the garden.
Cultivation Arizona cypress (*Cupressus arizonica*; hardy/Z 7–9) prefers light, free-draining soil. The fast-growing Monterey cypress (*C. macrocarpa*) tolerates sea spray, and makes a good specimen in mild coastal gardens. The Italian cypress (*C. sempervirens*) is hardier than its reputation suggests, and can be grown in cold-climate gardens. Stake trees for the first few years to assist root development.
Varieties *C. macrocarpa* (hardy/Z 7–10) is vigorous with bright green foliage and has a number of gold-leaved forms which require full sun to develop the best colour. Also try *C. m.* 'Goldcrest'; fastigiate forms of *C. sempervirens* (frost hardy/Z 8–10), such as

'Green Pencil', and members of the Stricta Group, which are slim and upright.
Uses Arizona cypress is often trained into triple-ball standards and corkscrews; Italian cypress is used as a vertical accent or for formal avenues, and Monterey cypress for architectural shapes.
Problems May lean or fall over if the root system is not well developed.

Euonymus
SPINDLE TREE

Evergreen forms of euonymus are useful topiary plants. They are salt and pollution tolerant, while *Euonymus fortunei* cultivars are tough, often developing pink tints after a frost. The white-variegated forms can be grown in shade and do not revert to all-green.
Cultivation Plants are easily grown on most well-drained soils. Avoid planting *E. japonicus* types in cold, frost-prone areas.
Varieties *E. fortunei* cultivars

Euonymus fortunei 'Emerald 'n' Gold'

Fagus sylvatica

(hardy/ Z 5–9) ,such as the variegated 'Silver Queen', 'Emerald 'n' Gold' and 'Emerald Gaiety'. *E. japonicus* (frost hardy/Z 7–10) and cultivars vary from the dwarf 'Microphyllus' forms to the larger- leaved, bushy cultivars, such as 'Aureus' and 'Ovatus Aureus'.
Uses Small-leaved forms of *E. fortunei*, as well as 'Microphyllus' forms of *E. japonicus*, can be clipped to form low hedging. *E. f.* 'Silver Queen' and large-leaved forms of *E. japonicus* make good clipped domes. 'Silver Queen' also makes a good wall covering. In mild areas, *E. japonicus* is used as a medium-sized hedging plant. Small-leaved *E. fortunei* cultivars can be trained as small potted standards.
Problems Scale insect. Leaf notching by adult vine weevils. Frost damage on spring growth of *E. japonicus*. Watch for all-green reversions on variegated plants.

Fagus sylvatica
EUROPEAN BEECH
A robust and relatively fast-growing hedging plant, it has broad, mid-green leaves that turn copper in autumn and last all winter.
Cultivation Full sun to part shade. Grows on any soil that is well drained, including alkaline. Trim or prune in early and late summer; the second cut encourages good autumn leaf coverage.
Varieties *Fagus sylvatica* has many forms, including purple leaf, fastigiate and weeping cultivars. American beech (*F. grandifolia*) has similar uses to European beech, but prefers acidic soil. (Hardy/Z 4–7)
Uses Suitable for formal boundary hedges and screens, and features such as arches, tunnels and *exedrae* as well as broad pyramids.
Problems Few, though can suffer from aphid attack.

Hebe
An evergreen New Zealand native. The many small-leaved species make dense, low domes in the wild; light clipping enhances the shape.
Cultivation Salt and wind tolerant, the small-leaved hebes are ideal for seaside gardens, but, with good frost protection, also perform well in cities. Grow on any well-drained soil in full sun.

Between late spring and mid summer clip lightly with shears, taking off just a few centimetres of soft shoot growth.
Varieties *Hebe rakaiensis* has light olive-green leaves; *H.* 'Red Edge' is light grey with a pink rim; *H. topiaria* is bright green, and forms a tight bun shape with little clipping. (Hardy/Z 8)
Uses Plant the dome shapes in a grid pattern to create a surface texture; use in a mixed border.
Problems In cold winters plants may be damaged by frost. Unless clipped annually foliage can develop gaps.

Hedera helix
COMMON IVY, ENGLISH IVY
With hundreds of cultivars, the range of leaf shape and variegation is staggering. *Hedera helix* has very flexible stems, making it ideal for growing over 3-D frames; it roots where it touches damp

Hedera helix 'Green Ripple'

moss, hence its popularity for chlorophyll figures. Plain green cultivars are best for geometric shapes that mimic traditional topiary.
Cultivation Plain green cultivars thrive in deep shade, but the more variegation, the more light is required. Drought tolerant when established, ivy prefers well-drained soil or potting mix. Wind the stems around supports and snip off excess growth; shearing is possible when grown over large topiary frames.
Varieties Choose small-leaved types of *H. helix* (hardy/Z 5–9 unless stated otherwise) with short joints (the space between the leaves), such as 'Duckfoot' or 'Très Coupé', which provide even coverage on small to medium-sized figures. Use faster-growing forms, such as 'Green Ripple' (frost hardy/Z 8–9), for swags and garlands. 'Glacier' (frost hardy/Z 8–9) has silver-white mottling and lightens a shady wall. Compact, brightly variegated forms – 'Eva' (frost hardy/Z 8–9), 'Kolibri' and 'Little Diamond' – create contrasting areas on moss-filled animal figures. *Hedera hibernica* 'Deltoidea' (hardy/Z 5–9) grows flat and even, and is useful for wall patterns such as covering trellis shapes.
Uses For 3-D topiary frames (quick substitutes for geometric forms); for moss-

filled or chlorophyll figures (either planted in the pot or directly into the moss); for wall decoration, trained free-hand or on wires; for creating swags and garlands.

Problems Under hot dry conditions, ivy is susceptible to spider mite. Spraying with water, as well as a cool shady position, help keep it at bay. Check potting mix for vine weevils. When old framed topiary becomes woody and threadbare, replant.

Hyssopus
HYSSOP

Traditionally used in knot gardens, this aromatic herb (bushy evergreen or semi-evergreen) is used to make low hedges. The foliage is dark green, glossy and needle-like and has spikes of blue blooms from midsummer.

Cultivation Tolerates thin, limey soils but must have good drainage and full sun. Clip either in midsummer or spring. Only cut back the new soft growth, not the woody base.

Varieties Herb nurseries should stock forms of *Hyssopus officinalis* with coloured flowers.
(Hardy/Z 6–9)

Uses Low hedges and edging, knots and small domes.

Problems Can get rather leggy with age. Discard threadbare plants.

Ilex aquifolium cultivar

Ilex
HOLLY

Many hollies are used for topiary and green architecture, and these evergreen shrubs or trees offer plain green or brightly variegated foliage to suit every size of garden. Berries are borne on female forms provided a male pollinator is nearby. Japanese (*Ilex crenata*) and Yaupon (*I. vomitoria*) hollies have very small leaves and closely resemble box.

Cultivation Grows in any reasonable soil. Plain green forms of common holly (*I. aquifolium*) and Highclere holly (*I. x altaclerensis*) are very shade tolerant. *I. crenata* 'Golden Gem' needs full sun to develop its yellow leaves. Ideally, shape large-leaved hollies with secateurs (pruners) or long-handled pruners rather than hedge trimmers to avoid half-cut leaves. Prune in spring and again in late summer if necessary.

Varieties *I. aquifolium* and forms (frost hardy/Z 7), such as 'Handsworth New Silver' (cream-and-pink variegation); 'J. C. van Tol' (green-leaved hedging); 'Pyramidalis' (compact upright cone); *I. x altaclerensis* (frost hardy/ Z 7–9) and forms similar to *I. aquifolium*, such as 'Golden King' (female; bright gold variegation and red berries). Compact, slow-growing hollies include *I. crenata* (hardy/Z 6–8) and *I. c.* 'Golden Gem', *I. vomitoria* (Yaupon; hardy/Z 8–10) and, for dwarf hedging, *I. vomitoria* 'Nana' (hardy/ Z 4–9).

Uses Forms of common and Highclere holly are used for hedging and large architectural features, as well as geometric specimens, such as cones, obelisks, mushroom-headed trees, cake stands and ball-headed standards. The latter may be grown in pots. Japanese holly makes small domes but can be cloud pruned or shaped into free-flowing forms. In America, the native Yaupon is a substitute for box in regions with hot summers, being clipped into shapes or used for hedging.

Problems Few, though common holly can be quite temperamental if it is cut back hard. Beware fallen leaves of prickly specimens when weeding.

Laburnum

The late spring or early summer flowering laburnums are well known for their bright yellow flowers. These fast-growing trees have soft, pliable young stems, making them easy to train over a framework. *Laburnum alpinum* 'Pendulum' produces pods of poisonous seeds which can be a danger to children, so try the safer *L. x watereri* 'Vossii' which has long, pea-like flowers. The foliage of both is light green and divided into leaflets.

Cultivation Easily grown in full sun. Tie to a framework and remove excess growth.

Varieties *L. alpinum* 'Pendulum' (hardy/Z 5–8), but better to choose *L. x watereri* 'Vossii' (hardy/Z 6–8) which flowers slightly later and has much longer blooms that cascade down through struts.

Uses Tunnels

Problems None, provided you use L. x watereri 'Vossii', which does not set seed.

Laburnum X *watereri* 'Vossii'

Laurus
BAY LAUREL, SWEET BAY

This popular evergreen bay is linked to Italian Renaissance gardens where it is used to make hedges and green architectural shapes, such as exedrae. With spicy aromatic foliage, this somewhat tender, large shrub or tree is commonly grown as a potted specimen at the centre of herb gardens. Paired standards can be used to frame a door.

Cultivation Well-drained fertile soil, in full sun. Good in mild seaside gardens where it can reach substantial proportions. Use secateurs (pruners) to avoid unsightly, half-cut leaves, and prune in the summer. In cold areas, stand pot-grown standards and spirals in a conservatory over winter, move to a sheltered corner next to the house or insulate well in situ.

Varieties *Laurus nobilis* has a number of varieties, but the species is the main topiary plant. (Frost hardy/Z 8–10)

Uses Lollipop-headed standards as well as spirals, cones, obelisks and hedges.

Problems Susceptible to scale insect, the first sign of which is often sooty mould on the leaves. Beware leaf scorch and frost damage in hard winters.

Ligustrum
PRIVET

Common privet (*Ligustrum vulgare*) has long been popular for everyday topiary with a menagerie of animals and birds emerging from the tops of hedges in cottage and suburban gardens. The glossy foliage will survive in all but the harshest winters, and, with frequent clipping, the leaves get smaller and the branching more dense, allowing for shapes with fine detail. *L. delavayanum* has recently become popular, its tiny leaves and pliable stems making it a good substitute for the slower-growing box in topiary frames.

Cultivation Fertile, reasonably well-drained, humus-rich soil, preferably in full sun, but will tolerate shade. Mulching with well-rotted stable manure aids growth as privet is notoriously greedy. Clip established hedges in late spring and early autumn or midsummer only,

Lonicera nitida 'Baggesen's Gold'

but clip topiary animals and other figures frequently during summer to keep them in shape.

Varieties *L. vulgare* (semi-evergreen which is suitable for hedging and topiary; hardy/Z 5–9); *L. ovalifolium* (hardy/Z 6–10) is similar with a number of colourful variegated forms, like gold-splashed *L. o.* 'Aureum'; *L. delavayanum* (tiny dark-leaved evergreen suitable for detail clipping and training over wire formers; hardy/Z 8–10).

Uses Hedging, arches and other architectural features, birds and animals. The small-leaved *L. delavayanum* is often grown as a round-headed standard.

Problems Semi-evergreen types may lose their foliage in cold winters. *L. delavayanum* needs protection in cold areas.

Lonicera nitida
HONEYSUCKLE

The shrubby *Lonicera nitida* is ideal for impatient topiarists because it not only looks like box but grows more quickly. Its drawback is that it needs more frequent clipping, and large figures may eventually become threadbare and wobbly.

Cultivation Grows on most soils in sun or, especially in the case of 'Baggesen's Gold', light shade, and is quite hardy. Tolerates salt spray. Having flexible stems, designs can be quite complex, but large pieces

are best trained over a frame for extra stability. Trim two or three times a year, as necessary.

Varieties *L. n.* 'Baggesen's Gold' has gold-variegated leaves. (Hardy/Z 7–9)

Uses For medium, round-topped hedges, simple geometric sculptures, such as balls and domes, as well as animal and bird figures, perhaps trained over wire.

Problems 'Baggesen's Gold' often reverts to all-green shoots which should be cut out at source as soon as possible. It can be scorched by strong sun on dry ground and harsh winters may defoliate the stems.

Myrtus
MYRTLE

Although it is not completely hardy, this glossy, evergreen, aromatic shrub is nevertheless still much sought after as a topiary plant. The small, dark green leaves are broad with an elegant point and, in summer, the dense, bushy stems are covered in tiny, white fragrant blooms that open from spherical buds.

Cultivation Best grown in containers so that plants can be moved to an unheated conservatory over winter. When grown in the ground, choose a warm, sheltered, well-drained spot on fertile soil. Clip in summer.

Varieties *Myrtus communis* and the cream-edged 'Microphylla Variegata'. (Frost hardy/Z 9–10)
Uses Balls, domes and small standards.
Problems Being slightly tender, winter protection is vital to avoid the cold and wet.

Osmanthus
FALSE OR SWEET HOLLY
Osmanthus has several tonsile forms (i.e. suitable for clipping) which, with their sweetly fragrant blooms, are ideal for the cottage or courtyard garden. The stems of the box look-alikes, *O. delavayi* and *O.* X *burkwoodii*, are also flexible, making it possible to train them over a frame.
Cultivation Grows on most soils including clay, and tolerates full sun or partial shade. Clip immediately after flowering, and as necessary during the summer.
Varieties *O. delavayi* and *O.* X *burkwoodii* both have small, dark green leaves and tiny, white spring blossoms. *O. heterophyllus* looks like holly and has attractive, variegated forms. (Frost hardy/Z 7–9)
Uses Hedging, standards, domes, mushrooms and for growing over topiary frames.
Problems Few, though some types need clipping regularly to avoid becoming shaggy.

Pinus
PINE
One of the principal plants for cloud pruning, pine has several species and cultivars which can be trained. Some have the desired aged look and, with additional training, such as wiring, can be shaped to form elegant tufts of pine needles on bare, curving stems.
Cultivation Pines are usually very tough and easy to grow on a range of soils. Japanese black pine (*Pinus thunbergii*) is drought tolerant and can even be grown on sand. The new growth occurs in pale coloured 'candles'. To shape the tree, remove the top half of the candles in spring to encourage side branching. Keep the ones you need and snip off the rest. Bamboo canes and wire can be used to train pines into more characterful shapes.
Varieties *P. thunbergii* (hardy/Z 5–8) for large, cloud-pruned trees in the ground or, for controlling the size, in containers; *P. sylvestris* 'Watereri' (for multi-stemmed, spreading cloud topiaries in large containers; hardy/Z 3–7); *P. mugo* (dwarf cultivars; hardy/Z 3–7) for domes and small, potted cloud topiaries.
Uses Cloud topiary; low hummocks.
Problems Soft young shoots may be attacked by caterpillars.

Pittosporum tenuifolium cultivar

Pittosporum
The New Zealand kohuhu (*Pittosporum tenuifolium*) has light green, wavy-edged leaves borne on black stems. Although the blooms are tiny and insignificant, most are fragrant. Variegated and coloured leaf forms are available, but they are less hardy than the species.
Cultivation Salt tolerant and ideal for mild gardens, it grows in any well-drained soil including ones containing lime. The species prefers some shade. Variegated and purple plants make good container subjects for large patio tubs. Trim to shape in late spring or midsummer. In colder gardens protect the roots from frost using a deep bark mulch.
Varieties 'Abbotsbury Gold' (gold marbling) and 'Silver Queen' (white variegation) are two of the best cultivars. The latter is relatively hardy and has a naturally compact, pyramidal habit. (Frost hardy/Z 9–10)

Uses *P. tenuifolium* can be used for hedging in mild seaside gardens, otherwise trim to simple dome or cone shapes.
Problems May be killed by frost in cold winters.

Prunus
LAUREL
The cherry laurel (*Prunus laurocerasus*) is a glossy, large-leaved plant, mainly used for hedging. The Portugal laurel (*P. lusitanica*) has smaller, pointed leaves on contrasting red stems, and is more versatile for topiary and a good substitute for the tender bay tree which is prone to cold, wet winters.
Cultivation Tolerates any soil, including clay, provided it is not waterlogged in the winter. Cherry laurel dislikes thin chalky soils, but the Portugal laurel is relatively lime tolerant. It is best to trim with secateurs (pruners).
Varieties *P. laurocerasus* 'Rotundifolia' is good for creating formal hedging; the

Pinus mugo

Quercus ilex

white-marbled 'Castlewellan' is less vigorous with a narrower leaf. *P. lusitanica* 'Myrtifolia' (and the variegated *P. l.* 'Variegata' are slower growing. (Frost hardy/Z 7–9)
Uses Ideal for creating quick-growing hedges and screens. Older specimens of cherry laurel can be converted into large dome or mushroom-headed standards. For tall, robust, round or dome-headed standards choose *P. lusitanica* or *P. l.* 'Myrtifolia'.
Problems Quite trouble free.

Pyracantha
FIRETHORN

Grown for its small, pointed, glossy foliage, creamy white blossom and heavy crops of ornamental berries, firethorn can also be clipped and trained to cover a house wall.
Cultivation Hardy firethorn tolerates a wide range of soils, including clay, but is unhappy on thin, chalky soils; will cover north- and east-facing walls.

Train on wires to form a network of horizontal branches. For improved berry displays, once the embryonic fruits start to develop in summer, cut back lateral shoots to expose them. Prune again in spring to remove some old flowering wood.
Varieties 'Golden Charmer' and 'Orange Glow' are two of the best for berries and most resistant to disease (both hardy/Z 6–9); 'Teton' (red; hardy/Z 5) is also good, although susceptible to fireblight which can transfer from hawthorn hedging.
Uses Espalier-style coverage of walls; wall-trained columns and clipped door surrounds.
Problems Ensure you pick scab-resistant cultivars like 'Orange Glow'. Birds eat all colours of berry. Hard pruning may sacrifice fruits.

Quercus ilex
HOLM OAK

Quite unlike deciduous oaks and looking more like holly, hence the species name, this evergreen is a useful plant for producing hedges and screens as well as large geometric shapes.
Cultivation Needs deep, well-drained soil and full sun. Use only young plants or there may be problems getting established. Grows well in mild coastal gardens although it is hardy. Clip in late summer.

Varieties *Quercus ilex* is the only suitable topiary species. (Frost hardy/Z 7–9)
Uses Hedging and green architectural shapes.
Problems Healthy, robust specimens have good natural resistance.

Rosmarinus
ROSEMARY

It is hard to believe that such an undisciplined shrub could ever have been trained into fanciful shapes, but, along with juniper, this aromatic herb was once widely used in topiary. Wiry stems are covered in tufts of narrow, dark green leaves and, in early spring, the species produces an abundance of pale grey-blue flowers.
Cultivation Grow on sharply drained soil or in containers, in full sun. Provide a sheltered spot in cold regions, such as against a warm wall.
Varieties *Rosmarinus officinalis* and *R. o.* 'Miss Jessopp's Upright' are the hardiest and most useful, the latter especially for hedging. (Frost hardy/Z 7–9)
Uses Medium-sized hedges, especially in mild gardens; small standards; simple geometric shapes (trained over wire frames).
Problems Brittle stems may break off during training. Vulnerable to frost.

Taxus
YEW

One of the best materials for producing sharp-edged, green architecture and geometric forms. The gold-leaved cultivars make a pleasing contrast against dark green. Irish yew (*Taxus baccata* 'Fastigiata') requires little training and is useful for marking entrances, creating avenues or when planted alone as an exclamation mark. Yew is poisonous to livestock.
Cultivation Grows on a range of soils provided they are well drained; drought tolerant once established. Sun or shade. Best planted in mild winter periods but, if planting in early summer, water thoroughly every two weeks during dry spells to aid establishment. Clip hedges and geometric shapes annually, ideally during the latter half of summer or, for really fine topiary, in the first half of summer and then again in early autumn. Irish

Taxus (gold-leaved cultivar)

yew produces multiple leading shoots which should be cut back when they start to elongate. Do not use yew for long-term container growth.
Varieties *T. baccata* (hardy/Z 6–7) has many forms and several gold-leaved cultivars, such as *T. b.* 'Elegantissima' (a golden yew with a broadly upright habit); *T. b.* 'Fastigiata' (narrow columnar habit); *T. b. Fastigiata Aurea* Group (gold form of species); *T. x media* cultivars (cross between Japanese and English yew; hardy/Z 5–7) and grown in the United States in place of *T. baccata*.
Uses Formal hedging (including buttresses and finials); geometric shapes, such as cones, pyramids, domes and obelisks. Yew houses and mushroom-headed standards; tunnels; organic, free-flowing hedging; abstract sculptures and figurative shapes.
Problems Avoid poorly drained soils as susceptible to phytophthora root rot. Not good in containers.

Thuja
ARBORVITAE
This aromatic conifer is used for creating formal hedges and green architectural shapes. It produces a fine, even surface when clipped. Western red cedar (*Thuja plicata*) has rich green foliage.

Cultivation Best on deep, moisture-retentive soil. Wind tolerant once established, but shelter when young using windbreak mesh. Clip once in late spring or, for extra control, again towards the end of summer. Do not cut back the leading shoot until the plant reaches its desired height.
Varieties *T. occidentalis* (white cedar; hardy/Z 3–8) and its forms, and *T. plicata* (western red cedar; hardy/Z 6–8) and its forms.
Uses Large hedges, screens and green architectural shapes.
Problems Trouble free.

Tilia
LIME, LINDEN
The soft pliable stems and quick growth rate of these hardy deciduous trees make them the perfect choice for pollarded screens which take up less room than traditional hedges, and allow more light through. Lime has large, pale or dark green, heart-shaped leaves and small fragrant flowers in summer. Though the common lime (*Tilia x europaea*) has a reputation for dropping sticky honeydew, other forms are safer. Flowers of *T. x euchlora* often intoxicate bees.
Cultivation Rich, deep, moisture-retentive soils are best. Prune during the dormant period, removing all growth not

Tilia

needed for training and which grows out from the horizontal supports. Remove suckers from the base of *T. x europaea*.
Varieties *T. x europaea* has now largely been superseded by *T. x euchlora* because it is resistant to aphids and doesn't produce suckers. Large-leaved lime (*T. platyphyllos* 'Rubra') has red winter shoots. (Hardy/Z 4–7)
Uses Pleached screens, formal avenues and covered walkways.
Problems Depending on the form used, aphids and suckering.

Tsuga
HEMLOCK
Western hemlock (*Tsuga heterophylla*) is a hedging conifer that is suited to warm maritime regions with a high rainfall.
Cultivation Western hemlock thrives on moist, neutral to acid soils. Protect from cold drying winds, especially when getting established. If the soil is limey, and the site exposed, try eastern hemlock (*T. canadensis*)

instead. Pinch out the growing shoots to encourage dense, bushy growth, and clip twice in the main summer growing period once the desired shape has been reached.
Varieties Eastern hemlock (*T. canadensis*; hardy/Z 3) and western hemlock (*T. heterophylla*; hardy/Z 6–8).
Uses Hedges and simple green architectural shapes.
Problems Suffers in polluted city locations and won't tolerate drought.

Viburnum tinus
LAURUSTINUS
This evergreen is a tough species with medium-sized, dark green oval leaves. From autumn to spring the plants produce a succession of white, honey-scented flower clusters.
Cultivation Tolerates any reasonable soil, and is happy in shade. Trim for shape after flowering, in spring. Standards may be trained from seedlings, but use rooted cuttings for the best flowering performance.
Varieties 'Eve Price' (compact and free-flowering), 'Gwenllian' (pink-tinged flowers and buds, less vigorous than the species), and the tender, cream-splashed 'Variegatum'. (Frost hardy/Z 7–9)
Uses Flowering standards, broad cones, wall-trained half cones.
Problems Sooty mould on leaves may indicate scale insects, aphids or whitefly.

index

PICTURE CREDITS

The publisher would like to thank the following garden owners, designers and institutions for allowing their gardens to be photographed for the purposes of this book. All photographs were taken by Steven Wooster, unless otherwise stated.

t = top b = bottom c = centre l = left r = right

Arley Hall, Cheshire 1; 3R; 32L; 35; 62TL
Athelhampton House & Gardens, Dorset 20-21
Bosvigo House 17
Chateau du Pin 4L; 27L; 30L; 40-1
Chenies Manor, Buckinghamshire 11; 24L
Elsing Hall, Norfolk 31B; 58TL
Elvaston Castle 59; 62BR
Fiona Henley Design, Hampshire 5R; 8–9; 27TR; 105BL; 57
Garden Picture Library 18L (J S Sira)
Ilford Manor 16 (photographer: Jo Whitworth)
istock images 28R (Aliaksandr Niavolin); 29 (Emilia Kun); 30R (Martin Bowker); 31R (Mostafa Hefni)
Judy Older, Kent 43R; 44 both; 50 all; 61
't Kragenhof, Belgium 12R; 39L

Leeann Roots 7
Mapperton Gardens, Dorset 25R
Parc Oriental, France 19L; 52–3
Peover Hall, Cheshire 25L; 32R
Piet Bekaert's Garden 6; 27R; 33L; 37
Renishaw Hall, Sheffield 12L; 23; 24R
RHS Chelsea Flower Show 1999 19R (Sculpture in the Garden)
RHS Chelsea Flower Show 2003 36; 38R (Topiary Arts Garden); 39R (The Romantic Garden Nursery)
Rodmarton Manor 10; 42L
Steve Manning, Bury-St-Edmunds 43R; 49 all
The Garden in Mind, Hampshire, designer: Ivan Hicks 26
Wollerton Old Hall, Shropshire 13R; 34R
Wyken Hall, Suffolk 13L; 22; 38L; 42R